SKIN FLICK

ALSO BY NORM FOSTER

NORM FOSTER

SKIN FLICK

PLAYWRIGHTS CANADA PRESS
TORONTO

Skin Flick © Copyright 2017 by Norm Foster

For professional or amateur production rights, please contact:
The Gary Goddard Agency
149 Church Street, 2nd Floor
Toronto, ON M5B 1Y4
416.928.0299, www.garygoddardagency.com/apply-for-performance-rights/

LIBRARY AND ARCHIVES CANADA CATALOGUING IN PUBLICATION
Foster, Norm, 1949-, author
        Skin flick / Norm Foster.

A play.
Issued in print and electronic formats.
ISBN 978-1-77091-777-4 (softcover).--ISBN 978-1-77091-778-1 (PDF).--
ISBN 978-1-77091-779-8 (EPUB).--ISBN 978-1-77091-780-4 (Kindle)

        I. Title.

PS8561.O7745S53 2017   C812'.54   C2016-907869-8
                                                 C2016-907870-1

We acknowledge the financial support of the Canada Council for the Arts, the Ontario Arts Council (OAC), the Ontario Media Development Corporation, and the Government of Canada through the Canada Book Fund for our publishing activities.

Skin Flick was first produced at Neptune Theatre in Halifax, Nova Scotia, from January 20 to February 15, 2009, with the following creative team:

Rollie Waters: David Nairn
Daphne Waters: Martha Irving
Alex Tratt: Gordon Gammie
Jill: Ginette Mohr
Byron Hobbs: Jamie Williams

Director: Walter Learning
Set and costume design: D'Arcy Morris-Poultney
Lighting design: Leigh Ann Vardy
Stage manager: Krista Blackwood
Assistant stage manager: Heather Lewis

CHARACTERS

Rollie Waters
Daphne Waters
Alex Tratt
Jill
Byron Hobbs

NOTE

Whenever Rollie steps out of the scene and talks to the audience as the narrator, the other actors freeze in place until Rollie steps back into the scene.

ACT ONE

Time: Evening. November.

Place: The home of ROLLIE *and* DAPHNE *Waters.*

It is a big older home that has been in the family for years. There is a couch, a big chair, a coffee table, and a telephone somewhere in the main living room. The entrance to the house is at stage right. The exit to the kitchen is at stage left. There is a stairway upstage left that leads upstairs and a hallway upstage centre that leads to another part of the house where the television is. As the lights come up, JILL *enters on the stairs, wearing a bathrobe. She is followed by* DAPHNE *Waters, who carries a clipboard and a pencil. They are followed by* ALEX *Tratt, who has a video camera. He is followed by* BYRON *Hobbs, who also wears a bathrobe.*

DAPHNE: Jill, come back. Please.

JILL: He was looking at my breasts! He was staring right at them!

ALEX: I'm the cameraman. I was looking at every bit of you. But it was strictly on a professional level.

JILL: Yeah, maybe with your camera eye it was professional, but your free eye was checking me out.

BYRON: I thought he was checking *me* out.

ALEX: I told you, I'm not gay!

JILL: What is it with you and breasts anyway? Do you have a fixation about them?

ALEX: I'm a man. Breasts are the Holy Grail.

DAPHNE: All right, look, can we go back in and continue shooting, please?

DAPHNE drops her pencil. She picks it up.

JILL: Only if he promises to stop checking me out.

ALEX: I don't see what the big deal is. After we finish this thing, your breasts are going to be checked out by thousands of men. Hundreds of thousands! They'll be the Super Bowl of breasts.

DAPHNE: Alex, would you just promise her, please?

ALEX: Fine. I promise.

JILL: Thank you. How did they look, by the way?

ALEX: How did what look?

JILL: My breasts. Were they pointing out or down?

ALEX: Straight out. Like laser beams. I think you fixed my bad eye.

JILL: *(to BYRON)* Is that true?

BYRON: They were looking right at me.

JILL: Daphne?

DAPHNE: They held me spellbound.

JILL: All right, good. Let's go.

JILL, ALEX, BYRON, and DAPHNE exit up the stairs. ROLLIE Waters enters from the wings. He is wearing a jacket or windbreaker of some sort.

ROLLIE: *(to audience)* Don't you hate walking in in the middle of a story? Well, that's exactly what you just did. Smack dab in the middle. So, let me back up a bit and fill you in on what's going on here. My name is Rollie Waters. I live here with my wife, Daphne. This was my grandfather's house. My father was born here and so was I. The house has been in the family for seventy-four years, and one day, by God, it's gonna be paid for. Daphne and I have a twenty-year-old son, Gerard, but you won't see him during the course of this story. He's off to university studying to be an architect. He doesn't know what's going on here because we don't like to bother him with our petty inconveniences. It might take his mind off of his keg parties and womanizing. So we'll just keep this quandary to ourselves. Now, the story began about two weeks ago. It was a Tuesday. I arrived home from work at the usual time, about ten past five. So that's what I'm going to do right now. I'll go out and arrive home and the story will start. I'll be right back. Oh, turn your cellphones off, okay? Because once we get going on this we don't want to be distracted. Thank you.

ROLLIE exits through the front door. After a moment he enters again. He is carrying a briefcase and a handful of mail.

Honey, I'm home! God, I love saying that.

ROLLIE takes his jacket off. DAPHNE enters from the kitchen carrying two glasses of wine.

DAPHNE: Hi, baby.

ROLLIE: Hi, Daph.

ROLLIE and DAPHNE kiss. DAPHNE gives ROLLIE a glass of wine.

DAPHNE: You did the "honey I'm home" thing again.

ROLLIE: I know. It's funny, isn't it?

DAPHNE: If you think so.

She takes the mail from ROLLIE and begins looking at it.

How was your day?

ROLLIE: Pretty busy.

DAPHNE: Oh?

ROLLIE: Yeah, the big bosses were in a meeting for most of the day, so they left me in charge of the office.

DAPHNE: That's nice.

ROLLIE: Yes, I ran a tight ship. I had them toeing the line.

DAPHNE: You mean Leonard.

ROLLIE: What?

DAPHNE: You had Leonard toeing the line. The seventy-five-year-old man you work with? The only other employee in the office?

ROLLIE: Right. I had his bladder-control garment working overtime.

DAPHNE: So, what was the meeting about?

ROLLIE: What meeting?

DAPHNE: The one the bosses were in all day.

ROLLIE: Oh, I don't know. Probably discussing how we can better publicize our product, which is theatrical wear. *(looks to the audience)* Costumes and such.

DAPHNE: I know what your product is.

ROLLIE: Pardon me?

DAPHNE: I know what your company does. Why would you say it like that?

ROLLIE: Just want to make sure it's clear to everyone.

DAPHNE: Everyone who? Who's everyone?

ROLLIE: Not important. And how was your day? How's the job search going?

DAPHNE: Oh, fine I suppose. I had those two job interviews today.

ROLLIE: Right. For the position of publicist *(looks to the audience again)* because that's your occupation.

DAPHNE: What?

ROLLIE: Nothing. Continue.

DAPHNE: So, I had the interviews but as soon as I walk in the room I can tell that they've rejected me before I even open my mouth.

ROLLIE: Well, Daph, you have to realize that a lot of companies don't want to hire a woman of your . . . uh . . .

DAPHNE: A woman of my what?

ROLLIE: . . . Height. Your height. It's a small woman's world out there, babe.

DAPHNE: Yeah, right. I understand what you're getting at though. If you're over thirty-five you're considered a dinosaur in the workplace.

ROLLIE: Thirty-five?

DAPHNE: What? I'm over thirty-five.

ROLLIE: And once again, you win.

DAPHNE: Oh, that reminds me. On your way home from work tomorrow can you stop at the video store and pick me up a movie? I have another job interview on Friday and they want me to write a one-page promotional blurb for a movie so they can see what I can do.

ROLLIE: Sure. What movie?

DAPHNE: Doesn't matter. Anything.

ROLLIE: Done.

DAPHNE: Thanks. Dinner will be ready in ten minutes.

DAPHNE moves towards the kitchen.

ROLLIE: What are we having?

DAPHNE: Spinach salad.

ROLLIE: Mmm. What else?

DAPHNE: Nothing else.

ROLLIE: Spinach salad? That's it?

DAPHNE: I'm on a diet, Rollie. Remember?

ROLLIE: You are?

DAPHNE: Of course I am. We're going to that charity auction next week and I want my Pucci to look nice.

ROLLIE: Daphne, your pucci always looks nice. You've got one of the nicest looking puccis I've ever seen.

DAPHNE: It's a designer, you tool.

ROLLIE: A what?

DAPHNE: Emilio Pucci. He's a dress designer. I bought one of his dresses last week.

ROLLIE: Oh. Expensive?

DAPHNE: You don't want to know.

ROLLIE: Actually, I do.

DAPHNE: It's an investment, Rollie. I plan to do some networking at this auction and I can't show up looking like Apple Annie.

So anyway, that's why I'm on a diet, and that's why we're having spinach salad.

ROLLIE: But I'm not on a diet.

DAPHNE: Yes you are.

ROLLIE: I am?

DAPHNE: Yes, you're on a solidarity diet. You're showing support for my diet by dieting with me.

ROLLIE: Oh.

DAPHNE: That's what spouses do, Rollie. When one spouse is attempting something difficult, the other spouse does the same thing in support of the first spouse.

ROLLIE: I see.

DAPHNE: Good.

ROLLIE: Daphne? I'm thinking of attempting some very difficult sex tonight. Just wanna give you a heads up.

DAPHNE exits to the kitchen. ALEX Tratt enters through the front door.

ALEX: Son of a bitch!

ROLLIE: *(to audience)* This is my best friend, Alex Tratt. He never knocks.

(to ALEX) Hi, Alex. What's up?

ALEX: I fucking got fired.

ROLLIE: You what?

ALEX: I fucking got fired.

ROLLIE: You got fired?

ALEX: I fucking got fired.

ROLLIE: *(to audience)* I should explain something. My friend Alex can have a bit of a filthy mouth at times. So, as I tell you the story, I'll edit out the really bad words so as not to offend the faint of heart among you. And I apologize for the previous outburst.

(to ALEX) You got fired?

ALEX: I ____ got fired.

He mouths the word "fucking" but no sound comes out.

What the hell?

ROLLIE: What's wrong?

ALEX: I just said I ____ got fired and . . . there it is again.

ROLLIE: There what is?

ALEX: What the ____ is going on? There it is again!

ROLLIE: Alex, just tell us why you got fired.

ALEX: Us? Who's us?

ROLLIE: Nobody. So, what happened?

ALEX: Well, get this. They sent me out on a story yesterday with Sandra Elkington.

DAPHNE enters.

DAPHNE: Hi, Alex.

ALEX: Hi, Daphne.

DAPHNE: What's new?

ALEX: What's new? I ____ got fired.

DAPHNE: What?

ALEX: I ____ got fired.

DAPHNE: You what got fired?

ROLLIE: He was just about to tell us why he got fired.

DAPHNE: Us? Who's us?

ROLLIE: Well, you and me of course.

DAPHNE: Oh.

ROLLIE: Go ahead, Alex.

ALEX: Well, they sent me out on this story with Sandra Elkington.

ROLLIE: The news reporter.

ALEX: Right. And we were covering the mayor's press conference.

ROLLIE: She was reporting it and you were filming it.

ALEX: Right.

ROLLIE: *(looks to the audience)* Because you're a television cameraman.

ALEX: Right.

DAPHNE: Rollie, why are you saying all this? We know he's a television cameraman.

ROLLIE: I just want to make sure the story is clear. Go ahead, Alex.

ALEX: So, we're covering the press conference and it's live and Sandra's wearing this blouse and you know how she likes to show cleavage.

ROLLIE: Oh, I know that.

DAPHNE: I hadn't noticed that.

ROLLIE: Me neither.

ALEX: So she's doing this live report and the director's in my headset saying that her blouse is too revealing. He wants me to tell her to close it a bit but she's doing the report, right?

ROLLIE: Right.

ALEX: And I can't interrupt her while she's doing the report.

ROLLIE: Of course not.

ALEX: So I've got the camera propped up on my shoulder with my right hand, and I zoom in for a tight shot on her face, and with my left hand I reach out and try and close her blouse for her.

DAPHNE: You what?

ALEX: Yeah, but she keeps slapping my hand away. So after she slaps me away the third time I go on the offensive and I slap *her* hand away. So we're having this little hand fight, you know, and the director's telling me to pull back because I'm in so close on her face that you can see the needle marks left by her last Botox injection. So before I pull back I make one last, desperate lunge to close the blouse and I wind up with a handful of breast.

DAPHNE: Oh my God.

ALEX: Yeah.

ROLLIE: You grabbed her breast?

ALEX: Yeah.

DAPHNE: But you didn't keep hanging on, did you?

ALEX: Not for long. So I pulled back and the blouse was worse than before and Sandra's got a flop sweat going now because of the hand fight and the mayor's watching us and the other reporters are filming *us* now and they showed the whole thing on the eleven o'clock news last night. It was a complete disaster.

ROLLIE: So, they fired you?

ALEX: They ____ fired me.

ALEX looks around, bewildered.

ROLLIE: Well, I'm sorry to hear that, Alex. What are you gonna do?

ALEX: I don't know. I mean, this couldn't have come at a worse time. I'm behind on my rent, I haven't paid my bookie in two months, and the phone company's threatening to cut off my phone. And if they cut off my phone how am I gonna place bets with my bookie? It's a conundrum!

DAPHNE: Maybe you can get hired on with another station.

ALEX: Yeah, right. What reporter is going to want to work with a cameraman who fondles them while they're on air?

DAPHNE: You fondled?

ALEX: I cupped! I just cupped it! And I didn't even know what I had.

ROLLIE: You don't recognize a breast when you feel one?

ALEX: When was the last time I was on a date? Huh? The last time I was with a woman? I don't know if I would recognize a breast if I was staring right at it.

He casts a glance at DAPHNE's chest. She crosses her arms.

ROLLIE: Well, you're gonna have to do something.

ALEX: I know. Could I have a beer?

ALEX moves towards the kitchen.

DAPHNE: Ah. Priorities.

ROLLIE: Help yourself, Alex.

ALEX: Thank you. And you know what really makes me mad?

ROLLIE: What?

ALEX: The guy who fired me? The news director? I got him his first job at that station nine years ago. Mother___.

ALEX mouths the word "fucker." He looks around, bewildered, and exits to the kitchen.

DAPHNE: Why is he talking like that?

ROLLIE: Like what?

DAPHNE: With those weird breaks in his sentences.

ROLLIE: I don't know.

DAPHNE: Well, I think it's very ___ strange.

She mouths the word "fucking" but nothing comes out.

What the hell?

ROLLIE: Let's invite him to stay for supper, Daph. It might make him feel better to be around friends tonight.

DAPHNE: You know he wouldn't be in this mess if he saved some of his money. But he gambles it away, drinks it away. He's very irresponsible.

ROLLIE: He's a bachelor, Daphne. There's no Mrs. Tratt, remember? He's only got himself to think about. When you're in this life alone you're pretty much unregulated. You're not tied down.

DAPHNE: Well, then maybe he needs a wife to show him what it's like to be tied down. Don't you say a word.

ALEX enters from the kitchen with a beer.

ALEX: Oh, and get this. When channel seven ran the story last night, the graphic underneath said, "Tit for Tratt."

DAPHNE: You wanna stay for supper, Alex?

ALEX: Oh, what, are you taking pity on me because I lost my job? Am I a charity case now?

DAPHNE: Yes.

ALEX: Okay. What are we having?

DAPHNE: Spinach salad.

DAPHNE exits to the kitchen.

ALEX: Sounds good. What else?

ALEX exits to the kitchen. ROLLIE speaks to the audience.

ROLLIE: And so that's when it all began. When Alex lost his job. Fast forward now to the next day. Isn't it great having a narrator like this? I mean, with a narrator you can skip over all the scenes you don't want to see. The three of us having dinner. Me watching a very informative and eye-opening documentary about the environment. Daphne and I making love. All right, we didn't make love. Daphne fell asleep. So the next day, things went from bad to worse. I arrived home at approximately the same time, so, I'll go out now and arrive home again. I'll leave my briefcase here this time. You've already seen me bring the briefcase in. No need to do that again. Just picture me carrying it. I'll be right back.

ROLLIE puts his jacket on, exits, and enters again. He is carrying a DVD. He is feeling sad.

Honey, I'm home.

DAPHNE enters.

DAPHNE: Hi, babe.

ROLLIE: Hi, Daphne.

DAPHNE and ROLLIE kiss. ROLLIE takes his jacket off.

DAPHNE: You forgot your briefcase this morning.

ROLLIE: I did? Oh. How 'bout that?

DAPHNE: Your brain was probably numb from watching that Three Stooges marathon all last night.

ROLLIE: Right.

DAPHNE: So, how was work today?

ROLLIE: Well, I've got some bad news, Daph.

DAPHNE: Bad news? What is it?

ALEX enters from the kitchen. He is carrying a beer.

ALEX: Hi, Rollie.

ROLLIE: Alex? What are you doing here?

ALEX: I'm out of a job, remember?

ROLLIE: What, you can't be out of a job at your own place?

ALEX: I need companionship at a time like this, Rollie. I need to be in the bosom of friends.

ROLLIE: Isn't that why you got fired in the first place?

DAPHNE: What's the bad news, hon?

ALEX: Bad news? You've got bad news?

ROLLIE: Yeah. Remember that meeting the bosses were in yesterday?

ALEX: No.

ROLLIE: I'm talking to Daphne.

DAPHNE: Yes, I remember. What about it?

ROLLIE: Well, it turns out it was a pretty important meeting after all. They've sold the company.

DAPHNE: What?

ROLLIE: Yeah, to a costume outfit in New York. And the new owners are moving the entire operation down there.

DAPHNE: Oh my God. They're moving?

ROLLIE: I'm afraid so.

DAPHNE: So, you're out of a job.

ROLLIE: Right.

DAPHNE: Oh, babe, I'm sorry.

ALEX: Is that a movie?

DAPHNE: Alex?

ALEX: What?

DAPHNE: Could you show a little compassion?

ALEX: Sorry. I feel bad for you, Rollie. I really do. It's eatin' me up inside. It's . . . What movie is it?

ROLLIE: Never mind. Here's your movie, Daph.

DAPHNE: Oh, Rollie. You lost your job and you still went out and got me a movie?

ROLLIE: Well, you needed it.

DAPHNE: Oh, you're so thoughtful. Thanks, hon.

ROLLIE: It's *Fun With Dick and Jane*. I just grabbed the first one I saw. I hope it's all right.

DAPHNE: It'll be fine.

ROLLIE: So, anyway, I've got two weeks left and then I'm done.

DAPHNE: Oh my God. So in two weeks we'll have no money coming in at all.

ROLLIE: That's what it looks like.

ALEX: Man, it kills me to see friends down on their luck like this. I'm gonna need another beer.

ROLLIE: Get me one too, would you, please?

ALEX: For you, buddy, anything. Hell, I'll let you have two if you want.

ALEX exits to the kitchen.

ROLLIE: It's my beer.

DAPHNE: Are you okay, Rollie?

ROLLIE: Oh, yeah. I'm sorry about this, Daph. I know it puts us in a corner financially.

DAPHNE: That's okay, baby. We've been in tough spots before. We'll work it out.

ROLLIE: But God, you know, at my age I should be settled. I shouldn't have to be worrying about finding a job. I should be enjoying the spoils of my years of hard work. Of a career. I swear, I thought the costuming trade was rock solid.

DAPHNE: Yes, well you also invested in the cardboard umbrella.

ROLLIE: It was recyclable. I thought it would sell.

DAPHNE: I know, baby. I know.

ROLLIE: Well, maybe you'll get that job on Friday and everything will be fine again. Huh?

DAPHNE: Right. Fingers crossed.

ROLLIE: And to that end, you'd better go and view that movie so you can write a fantastic blurb on it.

DAPHNE: Oh. All right. Or do you want some cheering up?

ROLLIE: No, you go and work. I'm fine.

DAPHNE: Are you sure?

ROLLIE: Definitely. Getting that job on Friday is the most important thing right now.

DAPHNE: All right, baby. I'll cheer you up tonight in bed. Okay?

ROLLIE: It's a date.

DAPHNE: Just don't fall asleep again like you did last night.

DAPHNE exits to the hallway.

ROLLIE: *(to audience)* I forgot she was going to say that.

ALEX enters from the kitchen carrying two beers. He gives one to ROLLIE.

ALEX: Here you go.

ROLLIE: I'll tell you something, Alex. I have got one spectacular woman.

ALEX: Who's that?

ROLLIE: Daphne!

ALEX: Oh.

ROLLIE: She's a saint. She's the kind of woman that you need.

ALEX: Well, believe me, if she wasn't married, I'd take a run at her. Yes, sir. A body like that? Woo.

ROLLIE: Alex?

ALEX: Hang on a second.

A beat as he pictures DAPHNE's body.

Oh yeah.

ROLLIE: Alex?!

ALEX: What?

ROLLIE: I meant you need someone *like* Daphne. Not Daphne.

ALEX: Well, there aren't too many like her out there, Rollie. God knows I've looked, but sometimes I think I was meant to be alone in this world.

ROLLIE: What do you mean? You've had some nice women in your life. Annabelle was sweet.

ALEX: Naw, I couldn't get past the name. Annabelle. Sounds like a circus performer. She'd get naked and all I could see were these big clown shoes.

ROLLIE: You pictured her in clown shoes?

ALEX: No. She really wore clown shoes. It was her "thing."

ROLLIE: What about Angie? I liked her.

ALEX: Naw. Every time we made love she wanted me to sing that Rolling Stones song in her ear.

He sings.

"Angie. Angie."

I can't be singing and making love at the same time, Rollie. I've got to be focused on the task at hand.

ROLLIE: Well, what about Teresa? I thought she was great.

ALEX: No, she loved me too much. She was head over heels.

ROLLIE: What's wrong with that?

ALEX: Oh, come on. How can any woman in her right mind love someone like me that much? There must have been something terribly wrong with her. So what happens now? With the job situation?

ROLLIE: I don't know. I don't know what I'm going to do. We haven't got a whole lot of money saved.

ALEX: Gee, there's a surprise. I thought you'd be pulling down top dollar at that funny dress shop.

ROLLIE: It's a costuming outlet. It's not a funny dress shop.

ALEX: They rent Porky Pig outfits, Rollie. Scooby-Doo. It's not Emilio Pucci.

ROLLIE: How do you know about Emilio Pucci?

ALEX: Rollie, come on. Look at me. You think I don't know fashion?

ROLLIE: Well, it was still one of the best costuming outlets in the city.

ALEX: You've been there a long time, huh?

ROLLIE: Sixteen years. And I had just worked my way to the top of the ladder.

ALEX: Over that septuagenarian you work with, right?

ROLLIE: Leonard, yeah.

ALEX: Well, no offence, Rollie, but that's not a very big ladder. It's more like a very wrinkly stepstool.

ROLLIE: But I was happy there. That's the main thing, right? I mean, we all aspire to work at a job we love, don't we?

ALEX: Yeah, I guess we do.

ROLLIE: You loved your job, didn't you?

ALEX: I did. I felt like I was born to have that camera on my shoulder. And I'm damned good at it too. But you grab one breast . . .

ROLLIE: Well, my job wasn't as glamorous as yours, but it had its moments. I remember this one time we had this producer come in who was filming a movie set in the sixties and he needed some sixties apparel immediately. Well we didn't have anything in stock because it was Halloween and a lot of kids were going as hippies that year. But I happened to be wearing a poncho and bell-bottoms that day so . . .

ALEX: Wait, wait. You were wearing a poncho and bell-bottoms?

ROLLIE: Yeah.

ALEX: Because it was Halloween, right?

ROLLIE: No, those were my everyday clothes. So, anyway, I took them off and I gave them to him right then and there. Stripped right down to my skivvies. That was also the day when I discovered that Leonard had a rather unhealthy interest in me.

DAPHNE enters from the hallway carrying the DVD.

DAPHNE: Rollie?

ROLLIE: Yeah?

DAPHNE: Take a look at this DVD for me, will you?

ROLLIE: Why? What's wrong with it?

DAPHNE: Just take a close look at it.

She hands the DVD to ROLLIE.

ROLLIE: All right, what am I looking for?

DAPHNE: Read the title. What does it say?

ROLLIE: *(reading) Fun With Dick—Fun with Dick?* What happened to Jane?

DAPHNE: Well, from what I saw, she's the one having fun with Dick.

ROLLIE: What?

DAPHNE: That's right.

ROLLIE: You mean?

DAPHNE: It's a porn flick.

ALEX: Cool.

ROLLIE: I'm sorry. I just grabbed the first one I saw. I thought it said Dick 'n' Jane.

ALEX: You thought it said what?

ROLLIE: Dick *and* Jane. I'm sorry, Daphne. Really.

DAPHNE: That's okay, hon. You had other things on your mind. I'll just take it back and get another one.

ALEX: Ah wait wait wait wait wait.

DAPHNE: What?

ALEX: Well, as long as you've got it.

DAPHNE: What?

ALEX: Well, I mean, you've got that big screen, ya know?

DAPHNE: Alex, it's a porn film.

ALEX just stares at DAPHNE.

Oh, God.

She moves past ALEX.

ALEX: Now listen, Daphne. Porn isn't just viewed by low-lifes, you know. It's viewed by Mr. and Mrs. Middle Class as well. People like you. *(points to DAPHNE)* And you. *(points to ROLLIE)*

DAPHNE: And you?

ALEX: I've been known to dabble in the cinema of the unclothed.

DAPHNE: Well, I think it takes a certain type to want to look at this filth. An undesirable type.

ALEX: Not always. Hell, married couples watch this material to spice up their sex lives. To bring their sexuality back from the dead.

ROLLIE: Why are you looking at me?

DAPHNE: Alex, I find that hard to believe.

ALEX: Daphne, it's widespread. It's a multibillion dollar industry.

DAPHNE: What?

ALEX: It is. *Deep Throat* has grossed over six hundred million dollars worldwide. And it only cost twenty-two thousand dollars to make. *Debbie Does Dallas* has grossed over a billion dollars and it cost a tiny fraction of that to make.

ROLLIE: How do you know all this?

ALEX: I'm in show business, Rollie. I read the periodicals.

ROLLIE: Yeah, right. I'll take it back for you, Daphne.

ROLLIE reaches for the DVD but DAPHNE pulls it back.

DAPHNE: Ah wait wait wait wait wait.

ROLLIE: What's wrong?

DAPHNE: *(to ALEX)* A billion dollars?

ALEX: Absolutely.

DAPHNE: And they cost very little to make?

ALEX: Next to nothing.

DAPHNE: Hmm.

ROLLIE: What's wrong?

DAPHNE: Rollie?

ROLLIE: What?

DAPHNE: I didn't want to tell you this because you've had enough bad news for one day, but, uh . . .

ROLLIE: But what?

DAPHNE: That job interview I have this Friday?

ROLLIE: Yes?

DAPHNE: I don't have it anymore.

ROLLIE: What?

DAPHNE: They called this afternoon to say the position has been filled.

ROLLIE: Oh no.

DAPHNE: I'm afraid so.

ROLLIE: Oh, man.

DAPHNE: And we do need money badly, and I'm thinking about this movie.

ROLLIE: I don't think they give refunds on rented movies, Daphne.

DAPHNE: No . . .

ROLLIE: I mean, how do they know you haven't viewed it?

DAPHNE: No, that's not what I'm saying.

ALEX: I know what she's saying.

ROLLIE: What's she saying? What are you saying?

DAPHNE: Well . . . no, it's probably a dumb idea.

ALEX: No, it's not. Go ahead.

DAPHNE: No, it's a silly idea.

ALEX: No, it's not. Go ahead.

ROLLIE: What idea? What?

ALEX: She wants to make a skin flick.

ROLLIE: What? You what?

DAPHNE: Well, if it's that lucrative.

ROLLIE: Daphne, you can't be in a skin flick.

DAPHNE: I didn't say I was going to be in it. Why can't I be?

ROLLIE: Well, because you're . . . I mean you're . . .

ALEX: Choose your words carefully here, Rollie.

ROLLIE: . . . Because you're my wife. And I don't want my wife having sex on film again.

ALEX: What?!

ROLLIE: Well, we rented a video camera for Gerard's seventh birthday party and later that night we had some wine and . . .

DAPHNE: Rollie? Do you mind?

ALEX: Why, Daphne, you little minx.

DAPHNE: Oh, cut it out.

(to ROLLIE) So, what do you think? I mean, how hard can it be to make one of these things? What do we need?

ROLLIE: Well, we need a camera.

ALEX: Got it.

DAPHNE: There, you see? We've got a camera and a professional cameraman.

ROLLIE: We need a location.

DAPHNE: We can shoot it right here.

ROLLIE: Here? In our house? In my grandfather's house?

DAPHNE: I knew your grandfather, Rollie. If he was still alive he'd want to direct it. Now, what else?

ROLLIE: Well, we need someone who would be willing to . . . you know . . . some actors who would . . .

DAPHNE: Right. Actors. Well, we could hold auditions. Isn't that what they do? Hold auditions?

ALEX: And what would you have these "actors" do at these auditions?

DAPHNE: Well, they could . . . you know? Show us how they . . . oh dear.

ALEX: Right.

ROLLIE: It would be an interview process. That's all.

DAPHNE: Exactly. We would interview them to find out what kind of experience they have. And we'd get a look at them to make sure they're photogenic.

ROLLIE: Oh! Oh! I just had a thought. I can supply the costumes.

ALEX: Costumes?

DAPHNE: Yes. Yes. And I could write the script.

ALEX: The script?

DAPHNE: Yes, something with a little romance in it. The story of a young woman who meets a fella. Maybe he's a soldier on leave and she owns a small Italian bakery, and he comes into her shop one day looking for a nine grain baguette.

ALEX: Okay, hold it!

DAPHNE: What?

ALEX: *(takes the DVD from DAPHNE)* Follow me.

DAPHNE: What for?

ALEX: I think you two need to see this.

DAPHNE: Why?

ALEX: Why? Costumes? Romance? Nine grain baguette? I think you need to see what a porn film is all about.

DAPHNE: I know what porn is all about, Alex.

ALEX: Really? Have you ever watched one from start to finish?

DAPHNE: Well no, but . . .

ALEX: Then let's go. Come on, Rollie. Showtime.

ALEX moves towards the hallway, stops, and looks back at DAPHNE.

Small Italian bakery.

ALEX and DAPHNE exit to the hallway.

ROLLIE: *(to audience)* And so we went to see what this type of film was all about. We have a fifty-two-inch screen. We were sitting five feet away from it. Forty-five minutes later, we emerged with a whole new outlook on the erotica industry.

ROLLIE stays on stage. It is now after they have viewed the movie. His expression is one of disbelief. ALEX enters.

ALEX: All right! I need a beer. Nothing like a good action film to work up a thirst.

ALEX exits to the kitchen. DAPHNE enters from the hallway, obviously shaken by what she has just seen.

ROLLIE: . . . Wow.

DAPHNE: That poor woman must be exhausted.

ROLLIE: And him. How could he . . . I mean . . . My God. That long.

DAPHNE: He certainly was.

ROLLIE: No, I mean length of time! For that long. That's a long time.

DAPHNE: Oh, don't feel bad, baby. I'm sure there was some editing involved.

ROLLIE: What do you mean, don't feel bad? What are you saying?

DAPHNE: Nothing. It's just that you were marvelling at the length of time.

ROLLIE: I can last pretty long.

DAPHNE: Oh, I know.

ROLLIE: Besides, none of that matters anyway. It's not size that matters, and it's not length of time that matters.

DAPHNE: . . . Well, what is it that matters?

ROLLIE: It's the quality of the work. It's like a piece of art.

DAPHNE: Oh.

ROLLIE: That's right.

DAPHNE: Well, then he just gave her the *Mona Lisa*.

ALEX enters from the kitchen with a beer.

ALEX: Rollie? It's your last beer? Okay if I have it?

ROLLIE: Be my guest.

ALEX: Thanks. Well, what do we think, folks? Still want to make this movie?

ROLLIE: I don't know, Alex. It's not really our cup of . . .

DAPHNE: If we make it, how do we get it out there? You know, distribute it?

ROLLIE: Daphne, are you really considering this?

DAPHNE: Yes, I am.

ROLLIE: A porn film?

DAPHNE: A cash cow. We need money, Rollie.

ROLLIE: Well, we've still got a little bit in the bank. At least we did the last time I checked.

DAPHNE: That was pre-Pucci. You have no idea how much that dress cost me.

ROLLIE: Well can't you return it?

DAPHNE: Silly boy. So, how do we get the movie out there, Alex?

ALEX: Don't worry about it. I know people.

ROLLIE: People in the film industry?

ALEX: Yeah, Rollie. People in the "film" industry.

DAPHNE: We'll need some start-up cash though, won't we? To pay the actors?

ALEX: Yes, we'll need that all right. That's a good point.

ROLLIE: Maybe we can get a government grant.

ALEX and DAPHNE stare at ROLLIE.

. . . What? The government is a huge supporter of the arts. Isn't it? . . . You mean it's not? Gee, I thought the government loved the arts. They always say they do.

(to audience) All right, that was a bit of self-indulgence on the writer's part. Sorry about that.

(to ALEX and DAPHNE) I'll get it.

The doorbell rings.

(to audience) Oops. I got ahead of myself there.

ROLLIE moves to the door and opens it. JILL enters. She is wearing a skimpy outfit and a top hat. She carries a bundle of balloons. She is missing the heel on one of her shoes and as a result she walks with a noticeable limp. She steps inside. She fumbles with a message card as she tries to read it and hold the balloons at the same time. Meanwhile, the top hat keeps falling over her eyes.

JILL: A poem for you on your . . .

Her hat falls over her eyes.

Crap.

She straightens her hat.

Can you hold these?

She hands ROLLIE the balloons.

All right. A poem for you on your birthday.

36

ROLLIE: Excuse me, but . . .

JILL: No, just lemme get through this, all right? Just let me get through it! Can you do that?!

ROLLIE: Sure.

JILL: Thank you. A poem for you on your birthday.

Michael, Michael, you're so hot.

JILL looks at ROLLIE. She doesn't think he's hot.

I'm so happy that I've got you.
And I thank my lucky stars above
For giving me your burning.

She looks at ROLLIE and takes a step away from him. She turns the card over.

Love.
And even though you're fifty-five
You still find ways to satisfive.

ROLLIE: "Satisfive"?

JILL: That's what it says.

ROLLIE: But that's not a word.

JILL: Hey, I didn't write it, slim. Okay? Now, can I finish the stupid thing?

ROLLIE: Well, actually . . .

JILL: So come to me, my birthday boy
I'll be your birthday cuddle toy
Let's have a little cowboy fun
I've got the holster for your gun.

Oh, please.

Love, Kim.

There. That's it.

(to DAPHNE) You Kim?

DAPHNE: No, not me.

JILL: *(to ALEX)* You?

ALEX: What? No!

JILL: Well I'm supposed to collect my money from Kim.

ROLLIE: I'm afraid there's been some mistake. There's no Kim here and there's no Michael.

JILL: What?

ROLLIE: I'm afraid not.

JILL: Well this is 32 Summit Street, isn't it?

ROLLIE: Yes.

JILL: And it's nobody's birthday?

ROLLIE: Sorry.

JILL: Oh, well this is just great.

ROLLIE: *(holding out the balloons)* So I guess you'll be wanting these back.

JILL: Can I use your phone?

ROLLIE: Sure. It's right over there.

JILL: Thanks. My stupid boss probably gave me the wrong address again. Idiot.

JILL moves to the phone and dials the number.

This is the third time this week this has happened. The third time! Yesterday, I walked in on a five-year-old's birthday party dressed like this. They were expecting Klutzy the Clown. Instead they got Slutzy the Tramp.

She looks at ALEX and his beer.

You got another one of those?

ALEX: Sure do.

ALEX starts for the kitchen.

ROLLIE: I thought you said that was the last one.

ALEX: No, I was saving the last one.

ALEX exits to the kitchen.

JILL: The line's busy.

She presses a button on the phone and hangs up.

God, what a day. First of all, my car breaks down and I've gotta take a bus here. And the driver's telling me to keep my balloons down because he can't see out the back window and I tell him to shove it and we get into this argument and he kicks me off the bus so I've gotta walk the last two blocks. Then I get my heel caught in the sidewalk out there and it breaks right the hell off. I would've fallen flat on my ass but the balloons held me up. And then I get here and it's the wrong address.

ROLLIE: Where'd you get your costume?

JILL: Hmm?

ROLLIE: Your costume. Where'd you get it?

JILL: Dorfman's downtown.

ROLLIE: I thought so. Amateurs.

JILL: What?

ROLLIE: Well, your hat's too big, your bottom isn't accentuated the way it should be, and your bosom needs to be pushed up.

JILL: Ya think so?

ROLLIE: Oh, definitely. Stand up for a second.

JILL stands. ROLLIE hands the balloons to DAPHNE and moves to JILL.

You see, the shorts need to be tapered under the cheeks to give them a natural lift. Right now they're hanging too freely. They're like two cloth sacks of Jell-O. And the bosom? Don't even get me started on the bosom. You want them pointing out, not down.

He grabs some fabric on the shoulder of JILL's outfit and pulls it up.

40

You see? Like that. That's much better.

JILL: How do you know all this?

ROLLIE: It's my business. It's what I live for.

ALEX enters with a bottle of beer.

Yes, give me a half an hour alone with you and we'd both come away satisfied.

ALEX: What's going on?

DAPHNE: Her bosom needs to be pushed up.

ALEX: Sweet. Here you go.

ALEX hands the beer to JILL.

JILL: Thanks.

DAPHNE: Can I tie these up outside?

JILL: Yeah, sure. Whatever.

DAPHNE exits out the front door with the balloons.

ROLLIE: I'm Rollie, by the way.

JILL: Jill.

ROLLIE: Nice to meet you.

ALEX: I'm Alex.

JILL: Hi. You look familiar.

ALEX: I do?

JILL: Yeah. Have I seen you somewhere before?

ALEX: No, I've just got one of those faces. Everybody thinks I'm someone they've seen doing something inappropriate.

JILL: No, I'm pretty sure I've seen you.

ROLLIE: So you work for a messenger service, do you?

JILL: Yeah, singing telegrams, romantic poems, heartfelt birthday greetings, all that shit.

ROLLIE: So have you worked there long?

JILL: Two months. I'm just doing it until I can get some acting gigs.

ROLLIE: Oh, you're an actress?

JILL: Uh-huh.

ROLLIE: Really?

JILL: That's right.

ROLLIE: Do you do films?

JILL: I do whatever comes up.

ROLLIE: Even better.

DAPHNE enters through the front door.

DAPHNE: Your balloons got away.

JILL: Perfect.

DAPHNE: I tied them to the railing out there and they just took off.

JILL: Don't worry about it.

DAPHNE: Rollie, they took the railing with them.

ROLLIE: Oh, great.

ALEX: I don't think your bosom needs to be pushed up.

DAPHNE: Yeah, and he knows bosoms. You might have seen him on the news the other night.

JILL: That's it! You're the guy who was fondling that reporter.

ALEX: I cupped! I just cupped it.

JILL: No, you held onto it for quite a while.

ALEX: I didn't know what it was.

JILL: You don't know what a breast feels like?

ALEX: Well I do now.

JILL: I think I'd better try my boss again.

JILL picks up the phone and dials the number.

ROLLIE: *(to DAPHNE)* She's an actress.

DAPHNE: She is?

ROLLIE: That's what she said.

DAPHNE: Well.

ROLLIE: So, what do you think?

DAPHNE: I don't know. Do you think she'd do it?

JILL: Do what?

DAPHNE: Nothing. Nothing.

ROLLIE: *(to DAPHNE)* You've got to work on that whisper voice of yours.

JILL: *(to the phone)* Larry, it's Jill. You sent me to the wrong address again . . . 32 Summit Street . . . Summit Avenue? No, you said Summit Street, Larry. Why in the hell would I write down Summit Street if you said Summit Avenue? . . . Incompetent? No, you're the incompetent one, you cockroach, you moron, you sleazebag, you jackass, you piece of crap . . . Fire me? What'd I do? . . . You haven't got the balls to fire me, Larry. I'm the cheeriest messenger there . . . Yeah, okay, you know what, Larry? You can go __ yourself . . . *(mouths the word "fuck" but no sound comes out)* . . . I said, go __ yourself . . . No, my phone's not breaking up. Why? . . . Ah, go to hell!

She hangs up.

Jerk.

DAPHNE: You're the cheeriest messenger there?

JILL: Problem?

DAPHNE: No.

ALEX: He fired you, huh?

JILL: Yep.

ALEX: Well, if it makes you feel better, I got fired yesterday myself.

JILL: Surprisingly, it doesn't make me feel better.

JILL pulls her hat down over her face and begins to cry.

I haven't got a cent to my name, I've got no car, no job prospects, and my breasts are pointing down instead of out.

She continues to cry and then takes a long drink of her beer.

Well, I guess I'd better hit the road.

JILL gets up and moves to the front door.

DAPHNE: Do you want me to call you a cab?

JILL: I don't have any money for a cab. I didn't get paid, remember?

DAPHNE: So how will you get home?

JILL: I'll walk.

DAPHNE: You can't walk with your heel broken like that.

JILL: No, I'm fine. All I need is a fife and a drummer.

She mimes playing the flute and walking like the famous fife and drum corps of the Revolutionary War.

ROLLIE: Wait!

JILL: What?

ROLLIE moves down and speaks to the audience.

ROLLIE: It seemed to me that this was too much of a coincidence to be a coincidence. It was as if this young actress in need had been sent to us. It seemed like a sign to me. I thought, "Maybe this was meant to be. Maybe by sending this downcast yet feisty young messenger someone is telling us to make this film." And she was a messenger! Get it? A messenger sent from above . . . or below. Wherever. And so I leapt into action.

He moves back into his previous position in the scene.

Wait!

DAPHNE: Rollie, you just said wait.

ROLLIE: I did?

DAPHNE: Yes.

ROLLIE: Sorry.

(to audience) When the narration gets too long I forget where I was.

(to JILL) Jill, is it?

JILL: Yes.

ROLLIE: Jill, we, uh . . . we might have a proposition for you.

JILL: What kind of proposition?

DAPHNE: Rollie, are you sure about this?

ALEX: I'm sure.

DAPHNE: Yes, I knew you'd be sure.

ROLLIE: I think it's in the stars, Daph. I really do. Jill, come back and sit for a moment, will you? We'd like to talk to you about a project we're working on.

JILL moves back and sits.

JILL: What kind of project?

ROLLIE: Well, it's a film.

JILL: A film? You guys make films?

ROLLIE: This will be our first.

ALEX: It's *their* first. I've been in the industry for years.

JILL: Yes, I've seen your work.

ROLLIE: So, we're about to embark on this project and we're looking for an actress to climb on board.

DAPHNE: Rollie?

ROLLIE: The part! Climb on board the part.

DAPHNE: Rollie?

ROLLIE: The role! An actress who can . . . Daphne, why don't you take it from here?

DAPHNE: Jill, we're making a porn film and we need a woman who would be willing to do something like that. Are you that woman?

JILL: . . . How much does it pay?

DAPHNE: Well . . .

ALEX: Five thousand dollars.

DAPHNE: Alex? We haven't settled on a fee yet.

ALEX: Well you don't expect her to do it for less, do you?

DAPHNE: Five thousand dollars?

JILL: It's not enough.

ROLLIE: What? It's not enough?

JILL: I'll do it for ten thousand dollars. Five in advance. And I want points.

ROLLIE: Points? What's that?

ALEX: She wants a percentage of what the movie makes in sales and rentals.

JILL: That's right.

DAPHNE: Well, we'll have to think about that.

JILL: Okay, you think about it. But I don't see any other actresses beating down your door.

JILL starts for the front door.

ROLLIE: Wait!

JILL stops. ROLLIE moves down and speaks to the audience.

She was right, and I knew she was right. We didn't know how to go about hiring actresses. We had no experience in that area. And it would be time-consuming. No, we needed to do this immediately. And don't forget, she was the messenger. The one who was sent to us. It was her destiny to be in this movie of ours. It was preordained.

ROLLIE moves back into his previous position in the scene.

Wait!

DAPHNE: Rollie?

ROLLIE: Darn it! Sorry.

(to JILL) We'll give you ten thousand dollars and two points.

JILL: Eight points.

ROLLIE: Four points.

JILL: Five.

ROLLIE: Done!

JILL: And I get to choose the guy.

DAPHNE: What do you mean?

JILL: Well there's going to be a man opposite me in this film, right?

ROLLIE: Oh, yes, I think he'll be opposite you at times, beneath you on occasion, perhaps behind.

DAPHNE: Rollie?

ROLLIE: What?

DAPHNE: She means co-starring with.

ROLLIE: Oh.

DAPHNE: *(to JILL)* Yes, there will be a man in the film with you. Of course.

JILL: Then I want to choose him. And it's not him. *(points to ALEX)*

ALEX: I'm the cameraman. And I just cupped it.

DAPHNE: I think we can agree to that. You probably know more about this than we do anyway.

JILL: Good. Then we have a deal?

DAPHNE: I think we do.

JILL and DAPHNE shake hands.

JILL: So, when can I get my five thousand dollars?

DAPHNE: Ah . . . well . . .

ALEX: You'll have it in a couple of days.

DAPHNE: She will?

ALEX: I've got an acquaintance I can contact.

DAPHNE: All right, you'll have it in a couple of days.

JILL: Good. I'll see you then.

JILL starts for the front door.

ROLLIE: Wait!

JILL: Again?

ROLLIE: Daphne, maybe you should give Jill a ride home.

DAPHNE: Good idea.

JILL: Are you sure?

DAPHNE: Definitely. We can't have our star walking home like that, now can we?

JILL: Well, thank you.

ALEX: Yeah, I'd better go too. I've gotta pull out the ol' Canon and dust it off.

DAPHNE: Excuse me?

ALEX: It's a camera. For the film?

DAPHNE: Oh.

ALEX: Such a dirty mind. I like that.

JILL, ALEX, and DAPHNE exit out the front door.

ROLLIE: *(to audience)* And so the wheels of porn had been set in motion. Now all we had to do was to find a man to play opposite Jill in the film. We notified some theatrical agents making them aware of what we were looking for and then we set up interview times for the Friday of that week. Daphne and Jill handled the interviewing process. I wasn't really comfortable sitting down with a man and asking him about his dimensions and about whether or not he had any special skills. Besides, it was a Friday—a work day—and I still had a job. Well, for another week and a half, anyway. Friday was also the day that Jill was to receive her five thousand dollars. Alex was looking after that. He said he had an acquaintance who could help us out in that area. Daphne and I weren't really sure who this acquaintance was, but we assumed he wasn't connected in any way to a reputable financial institution. And as you'll see, we were right. So, we'll pick up the story on Friday. We'll skip over Thursday. Nothing much of interest happened on Thursday. I went to work. I was told that the company wanted to take an employee to their New York office to help them get set up there. They picked Leonard. Our son Gerard called home and asked us to send him some money for textbooks. We didn't have any money so we told him to read over someone else's shoulder. And then Friday arrived. Jill came to the house and she and Daphne began the interview process. Daphne had instructed the prospective male leads to come through the back alley, climb over the chain-link fence that surrounded the yard, and then knock twice, then once, and then twice more on the back door. She didn't want the neighbours to see a steady stream of men arriving at our front door at half-hour intervals. She thought it might seem suspicious. Yes, having these men skulk through the back alley, scale a six-foot fence, and then give a secret knock on our back door would attract far less attention.

ROLLIE exits to the wings. DAPHNE and JILL enter from the kitchen.

DAPHNE: Well, what did you think of that one?

JILL: Didn't like him. He was too full of himself.

DAPHNE: Yes, he was a bit of a blowhard, wasn't he? And the last thing you want in a porn film is a blowhard.

DAPHNE and JILL exchange glances.

Anyway, we've only got one more to see so I hope he's the one. I mean, we're running out of options here.

JILL: I know. I'm sorry I'm being so picky, but I am not going to do this with just anyone.

DAPHNE: No, I understand.

JILL: I mean, I don't want a guy who's going to be leering at me the whole time. I want someone nice. Someone gentle. I don't want this to be dirty.

DAPHNE: Well, that's a lovely thought, Jill, but I think the whole point behind this kind of film is that it *is* dirty.

JILL: Well why can't we make this a different kind of adult film? Maybe there's a market out there for some tender sex. Something with feeling. Why does it have to be sweating and heaving and grunting and groaning? Bumping and thumping and thrusting and moaning. Screaming and scratching and pushing and rolling. What's so stimulating about that?

DAPHNE is lost in sexual thoughts.

Daphne?

DAPHNE: Please continue, dear.

JILL: It just bothers me that for some people their only image of intimacy is the kind of sex they see in a porn film. And now I'm going to be contributing to that image. I mean, there's something so much more arousing about a simple touch, don't you think? The way a man runs his fingers up and down your arm. The way he softly kisses your naked torso. The way he places his body against yours so gently that you barely notice the walls of intimacy being breeched.

DAPHNE: Can we get some air?

JILL: What?

DAPHNE: Air. Come. Let's sit in the backyard.

JILL: Are you all right?

DAPHNE: Fine. Yes. I just thought it might be nice to sit outside. Soak up the sun.

JILL: It's November.

DAPHNE: I know.

JILL: It's overcast.

DAPHNE: Well, with that gaping hole in the ozone I'm sure something ultraviolet will slip through. Now come. We can greet our final candidate as he scrambles over the fence.

DAPHNE and JILL exit through the kitchen. ALEX and BYRON enter through the front door. BYRON carries a briefcase. He is dressed in a suit.

ALEX: Hello? Anybody here? Have a seat, Byron. Go ahead.

BYRON: Thank you.

ALEX: No, thank *you* for coming here today. I know you've got a busy schedule and I appreciate you taking some time out like this.

BYRON: Can you tell me why I'm here now? I don't understand why you're being so secretive.

ALEX: Well I think I should let Daphne explain it to you. She's the one with the mind for business. Coming from me it might sound far-fetched.

BYRON: Does it have anything to do with the money you owe me?

ALEX: No.

BYRON: So you don't plan on paying me today?

ALEX: No.

BYRON: Seventeen hundred dollars, Alex. That's a sizable sum.

ALEX: It's huge.

BYRON: So you haven't got the money?

ALEX: No.

BYRON: A couple of hundred maybe. A show of good faith?

ALEX: Byron, I don't have it. I'm tapped out. Okay?

BYRON: Okay, that's fine. No problem. I'm sure you'll get it to me in due course.

ALEX: Due course?

BYRON: Yes, there's no rush.

ALEX: You know, Byron, you've got to toughen up. For a bookie, you're very soft.

BYRON: Well I don't like to be pushy.

ALEX: Well, at least once I wish you would threaten to hurt me or something. A broken leg. A twisted arm. A nose tweak. Anything. I mean, I have to respect my bookmaker, and, quite frankly, Byron, you're falling short in that area.

BYRON: I only got into this field because of my father, Alex. You know that.

ALEX: Your father, yeah. Ol' Wooden John. He was the best. You'd ask him for a break and he'd just give you that wooden stare. He'd look right through you. Make your blood run cold.

BYRON: Well, when he asked me to take over the family business I tried to say no, but gee whiz, he was so disappointed when I told him I wanted to be a doctor. I swear it broke his heart.

ALEX: Doctor. There's an easy profession. You get to look at naked women all day. I could go for that.

BYRON: You could?

ALEX: Absolutely.

BYRON: Hmm.

ALEX: What? What's wrong?

BYRON: Nothing. I just . . .

ALEX: Just what?

BYRON: I thought you were gay.

ALEX: You what?

BYRON: I thought you were gay.

ALEX: Yes, I heard you the first time. Why would you think that?

BYRON: Well you just have that lilt about you?

ALEX: Lilt? I have a lilt?

BYRON: You have a lilt.

ALEX: Byron, I bet on football. How can I be gay?

BYRON: I have several gay clients who bet on football.

ALEX: Yeah, well, I'm straight.

BYRON: Wow.

ALEX: I like the ladies and the ladies like me.

BYRON: Remarkable.

ALEX: And I do not have a lilt. There is no lilt. Let me find Daphne.

BYRON: Are you sure you can't tell me why I'm here?

ALEX: No. All I can tell you is it has to do with a movie and with actors' fees.

BYRON: Actors' fees?

ALEX: Yes. Lilt. Daphne?

ALEX exits to the hallway.

DAPHNE and JILL enter from the kitchen.

DAPHNE: Hello.

BYRON: Oh. Hello.

DAPHNE: Who are you? How did you get in here?

BYRON: Uh, I'm Byron. Byron Hobbs. Alex told me to wait here.

DAPHNE: Alex?

BYRON: Yes. Are you Daphne?

DAPHNE: Yes.

BYRON: Well, I'm supposed to talk to you.

DAPHNE: You are?

BYRON: Yes. About the uh . . . about the movie?

DAPHNE: Oh. You're here about that.

BYRON: Apparently I am, yes.

DAPHNE: I'm sorry. We were expecting you to come in the back way.

BYRON: The back way?

DAPHNE: But that's all right. You're here and that's the main thing. This is Jill.

BYRON: How do you do?

JILL: Hi.

DAPHNE: Jill is the female lead in the film.

BYRON: Oh. Congratulations. You must be very good.

JILL: I've never had any complaints.

DAPHNE: Well then, let's get right to the interview, shall we?

BYRON: Interview?

DAPHNE: Yes.

BYRON: I didn't know there was an interview involved.

DAPHNE: Well, we thought it was the best way to go. We want to deal with a person who has some substance to them. We don't just want a pretty boy with a big . . . resumé.

BYRON: I see. Well, all right then, what would you like to know?

DAPHNE: Well, I guess the first question is how proficient are you?

BYRON: How proficient am I?

DAPHNE: Yes, at the act of . . . at what you do.

BYRON: Uh . . . well, I'm fairly new to it.

DAPHNE: Really?

BYRON: Yes, I've only been doing it for about a year.

DAPHNE: A year? At your age?

BYRON: Yes, I'm what's known as a latecomer.

DAPHNE: Well, that's not bad.

JILL: No, I like that.

BYRON: But I learned from my father, and he was the best.

DAPHNE: Your father was in the business too?

BYRON: Yes. Ol' Wooden John.

DAPHNE: Wooden John? That's impressive.

BYRON: Yes, so I learned everything I know from him. Now, I must admit, I was a little apprehensive about it at first, but, well, I've stuck it out for this long, so maybe I'll stick it out for a while longer.

DAPHNE: Well, I think being able to stick it out would be a plus.

JILL: Definitely.

BYRON: I should tell you, though, there are those who say I'm too soft.

DAPHNE: Well that could be a problem.

BYRON: But I think when push comes to shove . . .

DAPHNE: And I'm sure it will, Byron.

BYRON: Yes, well I think when that happens I'll rise to the occasion.

DAPHNE: Well, you'll have to, won't you? Otherwise it could be embarrassing.

BYRON: Yes.

DAPHNE: You don't want to appear too malleable in that area.

BYRON: No, ma'am, I certainly don't want that.

They laugh.

DAPHNE: I think you know what I'm saying.

BYRON: I think I do.

DAPHNE: You know, you're different from most men in your field, Byron. You have a humble quality about you. Don't you think, Jill?

JILL: Yes. It's very refreshing.

BYRON: Well, I've never been one to brag. I mean, there's nothing worse than overselling yourself only to come up short.

DAPHNE: But you're not opposed to a challenge, I hope.

BYRON: No, not at all. I'm sorry. Is there a challenge involved here?

DAPHNE: Well I'd say there is, yes. It could be quite arduous at times.

BYRON: Arduous?

DAPHNE: Yes, I mean I know it sounds fairly straightforward— enjoyable even—but it could be exhausting. It could be a lot of hard work.

BYRON: Well we have a saying where I come from . . .

DAPHNE: And where's that?

BYRON: Pardon me?

DAPHNE: Where do you come from?

BYRON: I was born three blocks up.

DAPHNE: Ah.

BYRON: And we have a saying up there. We say, "If it's not hard, it's not worth doing."

DAPHNE: We have the same saying at my women's group.

ALEX enters from the hallway.

ALEX: Oh, there you are.

DAPHNE: Hi, Alex.

ALEX: I see you've met Byron.

DAPHNE: Yes, we have. We've been having a very nice chat.

ALEX: So you explained everything to him?

DAPHNE: Yes. Everything.

BYRON: Actually, I'm still rather confused. I don't know why I'm here exactly.

ALEX: What?

DAPHNE: What do you mean you don't know why you're here?

ALEX: I thought you said you explained everything to him.

DAPHNE: I did.

(to BYRON) You're here for the movie, right?

BYRON: Well that's what Alex said.

DAPHNE: *(to ALEX)* You see? He wants to be in the movie.

ALEX: *In* the movie? No, he's not here to be in it. He's the money man.

DAPHNE: He's the what?

BYRON: I'm the what?

ALEX: Byron, we're making a porn film and we need you to back us financially.

BYRON: A porn film?!

ALEX: Yes. God, Daphne, how could you mistake this guy for a porn actor? He's my bookie. He doesn't know the first thing about acting. Or sex for that matter.

DAPHNE: Oh.

(to BYRON) I'm terribly sorry.

BYRON: No, I know about sex. It's just that I'm kind of shy and I have trouble approaching women, that's all.

DAPHNE: I meant I'm sorry for the misunderstanding.

BYRON: Oh.

ALEX: Boy. Byron in a porn film? What do you think of that, Byron? Is that nuts or what?

BYRON: Yes, it's outrageous all right.

ALEX: I mean, no offence, but who's gonna pay to see that?

BYRON: Right.

DAPHNE: *(to BYRON)* Well, now that we've cleared that up, maybe we should talk about the real reason you're here.

JILL: He's the one.

DAPHNE: What?

JILL: *(pointing at BYRON)* He's the one. I want him.

Lights down.

End of Act One.

ACT TWO

Time: Three days later. Monday.

Place: The same.

Lights come up and ALEX enters from the wings. He speaks to the audience.

ALEX: Hi. Welcome back. You ready to hear the rest of the story? Good. Okay, so, even though there was some confusion as to why Byron was at the house that day, he was subsequently hired to play opposite Jill in our movie.

ROLLIE enters from the wings. He looks at ALEX for a moment.

Now this was a whole new experience for Byron. I mean, he was a bookie, right? And now he's starring in an X-rated movie.

ROLLIE: Alex?

ALEX: Hmm? What?

ROLLIE: What are you doing?

ALEX: I'm telling the story.

ROLLIE: But I was telling the story.

ALEX: Yeah, but you wouldn't let me say "fuck."

ROLLIE: No, I wouldn't. Now go. Leave.

ALEX: That's censorship, Rollie. Censorship is a very slippery slope. I don't think you want to start down that road.

ROLLIE: Would you just go, please?

ALEX: All right, fine. But if nobody swears in this thing we won't be taken seriously.

ROLLIE: Oh don't be ridiculous.

ALEX: It's true. There are those out there—you know, academics and critics and such—who need an angst-ridden story filled with expletives. Otherwise they think it's "light." That's all I'm sayin'.

ALEX exits to the wings.

ROLLIE: *(to audience)* Sorry about that. And now back to my story. As Alex mentioned, Byron agreed to play opposite Jill in the film. I'm not really sure why. There could have been a number of reasons, I suppose. Maybe he wanted to break out of that shell of his. Do something wild for a change. Maybe he was flattered that Jill wanted him for the part and he couldn't say no to her. Or maybe he was very inexperienced sexually and he was looking for some on-the-job training. So we're going to jump ahead to Monday now. Three days later. I was at work, of course, into my last week of employment there, but the others were at the house for the first day of shooting. We had a title for the film now, after much debate on the subject. Alex suggested *Diddler on the Roof.* That was summarily dismissed. I came up with *Die Hard,* but, again, that was rejected. And finally, Daphne, the voice of reason, came up with our working title. *Dr. Toolittle.* It would be the story of a doctor, played by Byron, who has a uh . . . physical deficiency, and his nurse, played by Jill, who helps him overcome his shortage. I don't know where Daphne came up with that idea. It's so far removed from what she's accustomed to. So on that first day, Daphne had scheduled a dry run where she would walk the actors through the story and explain to them what she wanted from them. I should warn you that this next segment might be a tad risqué. If you have a blood-pressure problem or a bad ticker, this could be hazardous, so please, view it at your own peril.

ROLLIE exits to the wings. DAPHNE, ALEX, JILL, and BYRON enter on the stairs. ALEX has a video camera on his shoulder. DAPHNE has a clipboard and a pencil. JILL is dressed as a nurse and BYRON as a doctor.

DAPHNE: All right, Jill, Byron, we'll start with you two on the couch here. Jill, you sit to Byron's right, please.

JILL and BYRON sit on the couch.

Good. Is that going to play, Alex?

ALEX: Yeah, that'll work. I'll open with a two shot and then zoom in for the close-ups.

BYRON: Will we be wearing makeup for the close-ups on our faces?

ALEX: I'm sorry. Did I mention faces?

DAPHNE: All right, now this is where the first encounter will take place between the two of you. You will begin here, maybe have sex in a couple of positions on the couch, and then we'll move into the shower for some wet sex.

BYRON: So we're going to be engaging in the act of love here?

DAPHNE: That's right, boobala.

BYRON: Uh-huh. Isn't this supposed to be the doctor's office?

DAPHNE: Yes, it is, yes.

BYRON: Well, a doctor and his nurse having relations in his office, isn't there something morally ambiguous about that? I mean, there are probably patients in the waiting room who need immediate medical attention. They might have a kidney stone. Dysentery. An impacted bowel. And I'm in here being pleasured. Isn't that unethical?

DAPHNE: . . . It's after-hours.

BYRON: Oh.

DAPHNE: The office is closed. There are no patients. No impacted bowels. Nothing.

BYRON: Good. Good. Because if I feel torn morally then I might not be able to, you know . . . get the rocket off the launch pad.

DAPHNE: No, you're okay. All systems go.

BYRON: Good.

DAPHNE: Alex, you're mapping your shots?

ALEX: All set.

ALEX looks through his camera to practise what he will be shooting.

DAPHNE: So here's what's going to happen. It's the end of the day and the two of you are on the couch and the nurse says something like, "Wow, what a long . . . day, Doctor." And the doctor says, "Yes, it was a long day, Nurse." And the nurse says, "But we certainly helped a lot of people, didn't we, Doctor?" And the doctor says, "We certainly did, Nurse." And the nurse says . . .

ALEX: Mother of God!

DAPHNE: What?

ALEX: Your dialogue is death. Three people just walked out. Come on, let's get to the action.

DAPHNE: I'm just trying to give the moment some underpinning.

ALEX: Some what?

DAPHNE: Underpinning. I'm trying to lay a foundation.

ALEX: All right, lay, good. Foundation, bad.

DAPHNE: Fine. So they have a very brief conversation and then, Byron, you'll place your hand on Jill's breast.

BYRON: Pardon me?

DAPHNE: You'll put your hand on Jill's breast. Could you do that now, please? I want to see how it looks.

BYRON: Why would I put my hand on her breast?

DAPHNE: Well, because you want to have sex with her.

BYRON: Yes, I understand that, but to just lunge for a breast out of the blue, isn't that unrealistic?

ALEX: You want me to show him how it's done?

DAPHNE: No. Byron, just put your hand on her breast, please.

BYRON: But with no sweet-talk beforehand? Like, "Oh, you're so pretty." Or, "Oh, can I touch your breast?" Nothing like that?

DAPHNE: No. Now grab the boob, please.

BYRON: All right.

He puts his hand out towards JILL, then pulls it back.

In which manner? Am I grabbing the entire breast in a groping fashion? Am I merely cupping it underneath? I'm not clear on what you're asking for.

ALEX: Are you sure you don't want me to show him?

DAPHNE: Byron, please. Just touch the breast any way you want to.

JILL: It's okay, Byron. Go ahead.

BYRON hesitates.

Really. It's okay.

BYRON: All right then.

BYRON moves his hand towards JILL's breast and then stops.

I need a mint. Does anyone have a mint?

DAPHNE: A what, darling?

BYRON: A breath mint. I need a breath mint.

ALEX: You're fondling her. You need a mint to fondle?

DAPHNE: Here, Byron. I've got some.

DAPHNE takes a package of mints out of her pocket and hands them to BYRON.

BYRON: Thank you. *(looks at the package)* Oh, green tea mints. I've never tried these before.

BYRON takes a mint and hands the package back to DAPHNE.

ALEX: Green tea mints?

DAPHNE: What's wrong?

ALEX: You want your breath to smell like old tea? What, you couldn't find any cabbage flavoured mints?

DAPHNE: All right, Byron. Are we all set now?

BYRON: I believe so, yes.

DAPHNE: Good. Now place your hand on Jill's breast, please.

BYRON holds his hand out hesitantly and JILL suddenly leans forward and puts her breast against BYRON's hand.

BYRON: *(to DAPHNE)* How's that?

DAPHNE: Well, it's actually pretty sterile. Jill, how does that strike you?

JILL: I'm not excited by it.

BYRON: I'm sorry.

JILL: No, it's not you.

BYRON: I'm new to this.

JILL: You're doing fine.

BYRON: Thank you. You're very kind.

ALEX: Maybe he should reach inside the top when he grabs the breast?

DAPHNE: Say again?

ALEX: Can he reach inside her top? I think it would make for a more interesting shot.

DAPHNE: Sure, we can try that. Byron, can you reach inside the top, please?

BYRON: I'm sorry?

DAPHNE: When you touch the breast, can you put your hand inside her top, please?

BYRON: Uh . . . sure. I suppose I can do that. I . . . Just reach inside?

DAPHNE: Right.

BYRON: Okay. So I'll just slide it right in the, uh . . . Could I have a glass of water, please?

DAPHNE: Water?

BYRON: Yes, I'm a little dry. It's very dry in here.

DAPHNE: Alex, can you get him a glass of water, please? Thank you.

ALEX exits to the kitchen.

BYRON: *(to JILL)* I have a problem with dryness. My throat seizes up and I feel like I'm going to choke . . . you know . . . I gag. My skin gets dry too. Very dry. I go through moisturizer likes it's canola oil. I cook a lot so I go through a lot of canola. Do you exfoliate, because your face is very smooth. Like a baby's bottom. Well, I'm not saying your face looks like a baby's bottom. I'm not comparing your face to a toddler's buttocks. I just mean it's smooth, as opposed to my skin, which is like alligator skin. You could make luggage out of my skin. I could be a handbag.

ALEX enters with a glass of water.

ALEX: Here you go.

BYRON: Oh, thank you. Thank you very much.

BYRON takes the glass of water and drinks as the others stare at him.

Ah! That's better.

DAPHNE: All set now?

BYRON: All set.

DAPHNE: Good. Now reach inside the nurse's top and touch her breast, please.

BYRON: Right.

(to JILL) Well, here goes. No turning back now . . . We're diving right in, as they say . . . Goin' for broke.

DAPHNE: Byron?!

BYRON: Right. Here goes then.

BYRON reaches his hand inside JILL's top. She screams and he pulls his hand out again.

JILL: Yeow!

BYRON: What? What's wrong?

JILL: Your hand is freezing cold.

BYRON: Oh, that's the hand I held the glass of water with. I'm sorry.

BYRON blows on his hand to warm it up.

DAPHNE: All right, look, let's jump ahead, shall we? You've touched her breast, you've undressed each other, and now you're making love. Can we try a couple of positions, please?

JILL stands up and begins stretching.

JILL: Which ones?

DAPHNE: Pardon me?

JILL: Which positions?

DAPHNE: Well, how many do you know?

JILL: Well, uh . . .

JILL begins counting in her head. As she counts she puts up a finger for each position she thinks of. She goes though about twenty.

DAPHNE: Yes, okay, Jill. Thank you. Byron . . .

DAPHNE looks at JILL who is still counting. She takes JILL's hand and puts it down at JILL's side.

Thank you, Jill. Byron, how many do you know?

BYRON: Uh . . . *(pointing to JILL's hands)* The first two there.

DAPHNE: All right, look, let's start off with something relatively innocent.

ALEX: Innocent?

DAPHNE: Yes. I don't want to get too kinky here. I mean, sure, it's a porn film, but I don't want it to be degrading to women.

There is a pause, and then the four of them break into hysterical laughter.

ALEX: That's a good one.

DAPHNE: All right, Jill, why don't you straddle Byron for me?

JILL: Okay.

JILL sits astride BYRON's lap, facing away from him, looking out towards the audience.

How's this?

DAPHNE: Well, that can't work, can it?

JILL: Sure it can.

DAPHNE examines the position for a moment.

·**DAPHNE:** Do you think so? Wouldn't you have to be facing him?

JILL: No. You can do it this way.

DAPHNE: Really? Alex? What do you think? Would that work?

BYRON: Actually, it's working already.

DAPHNE: All right. Let's see then. What next? Oh, I know! I know! So you'll do it like that for a while and then Byron, can you stand up while holding onto Jill's waist?

BYRON: Stand up?

DAPHNE: Yes, I want you to stand up, lifting Jill with you and then turn around and bend her over the couch.

ALEX: Oh, good call, Daphne.

DAPHNE: Can you do that, Byron?

BYRON: Uh . . . well, I'll try. Uh . . .

(to JILL) Ready?

JILL: All set.

BYRON stands, holding onto JILL's waist. They move awkwardly and unsteadily. JILL winds up with her hands on the coffee table to steady herself. BYRON winds up holding onto JILL's legs. They hold that wheelbarrow-like pose for a moment.

DAPHNE: The couch, Byron. The couch.

BYRON turns JILL around but JILL's hands are still on the coffee table. She directs BYRON with one hand, motioning him towards the couch. She makes it to the couch. Finally, awkwardly, she tumbles over the back of the couch and disappears from sight.

Jill, are you all right?

JILL stands up from behind the couch.

JILL: Oh yeah. I'm good.

ALEX: Well, that was sexy.

BYRON: I think the problem is the couch.

DAPHNE: Pardon me?

BYRON: The couch. There's not a whole lot of room. It's very limiting.

DAPHNE: Hmm. Jill? What do you think?

JILL: Well, the couch is okay for a few positions but if you want to run through the whole repertoire then we're definitely gonna need more room.

DAPHNE: I see.

JILL: A lot more.

DAPHNE: Right.

JILL: We might have to push two king-size beds together.

ALEX: Okay, now I need some water.

DAPHNE: All right, look, let's forget about the couch. We'll do it in the bedroom.

ALEX: Really?

DAPHNE: Well, we'll have to.

ALEX: In the bed where you and Rollie sleep?

DAPHNE: Yes. Why?

ALEX: Where you and Rollie . . . you know?

DAPHNE: Sheets can be washed, Alex. Or burned. Now, I'm going to have to rethink this whole scene.

(to JILL and BYRON) We'll call you two when we're ready. And this time we'll be shooting for real. Alex? On me.

ALEX: Yes, ma'am.

DAPHNE and ALEX exit up the stairs.

BYRON: Shooting for real.

JILL: Yep.

BYRON: I'm sorry about the couch thing.

JILL: That's okay.

BYRON: I'll try and be more careful from now on.

JILL: Don't worry about it.

BYRON: I'm a little nervous, I guess. I'm out of my element here. This isn't really my bailiwick, you know? Acting. Having sex.

JILL: So, you really haven't done it much?

BYRON: Once. A high school production of *Oklahoma!*.

JILL: I meant the sex.

BYRON: So did I.

JILL: So you haven't had a girlfriend since then?

BYRON: No, I had a girlfriend. But no sex. She said she was saving herself for marriage. Turned out she was saving herself for a truck driver from Chicoutimi. She broke up with me over his two-way radio. She said we were over. And out.

JILL: And you didn't see it coming?

BYRON: No. Not at all. In fact, I was like God to her.

JILL: Really?

BYRON: Oh yeah. She'd say things like, "God, you're so stupid."

JILL: That's funny.

BYRON: Well, you have to be able to laugh about these things, right?

JILL: Right.

BYRON: What about you? No boyfriend?

JILL: Not right now. I was seeing this one guy for a couple of years but we broke it off a few months ago.

BYRON: Oh. What happened?

JILL: Nothing. We just decided it was time to move on.

BYRON: So it was a mutual parting of the ways.

JILL: Right.

BYRON: Uh-huh.

JILL: What's wrong?

BYRON: Nothing. It's just that I think there's always one person who does a little more of the leaving than the other. But I suppose it's possible to be equally agreeable about a breakup sometimes. I mean, what do I know?

JILL: It was him. He did more of the leaving.

BYRON: I see.

JILL: Actually, he did all of the leaving.

BYRON: Was it another woman?

JILL: No. It was just me. I guess I wasn't the one. You men are always looking for "the one," isn't that right?

BYRON: What? No?

JILL: You're not?

BYRON: No, I thought it was women who were always looking for "the one."

JILL: No. We're just looking for *someone*. We're not looking for *the* one.

BYRON: Oh.

JILL: Yeah, we find *someone* and then we change him into *the* one. It didn't work on my last guy, though. He was trying to change *me*.

BYRON: What didn't he like about you?

JILL: I don't know. Out-of-work actress, chip on my shoulder, unusually lengthy PMS. I thought that spelled dream girl. But it's okay. I don't mind being on my own.

BYRON: No, I don't mind being alone either.

JILL: No one to answer to.

BYRON: You can come and go as you please.

JILL: No one else's feelings to consider.

BYRON: You do what makes *you* happy.

JILL: No one hogging the covers in bed.

BYRON: Because you're in bed all by yourself.

JILL and BYRON think about this for a moment.

JILL: Yeah, we're much better off.

BYRON: Absolutely.

Beat.

So, have you done many of these types of films?

JILL: This is my first.

BYRON: Really? That surprises me.

JILL: Why?

BYRON: Well, you don't seem too inhibited. You seem pretty relaxed.

JILL: Yeah, well, we haven't gotten naked yet. Being naked in front of a camera is going to be a whole different story.

BYRON: Are you worried about that?

JILL: Are you kidding? I haven't worked out in a while. When the clothes come off there's no telling where things will fall.

BYRON: I think you've got a lovely body.

JILL: You do?

BYRON: I think it's beautiful.

JILL: Well thank you.

BYRON: It will be an honour to be on top of it.

JILL: Well, aren't you sweet?

BYRON: I'm just being truthful.

JILL: . . . So, you're a bookie, huh?

BYRON: Yeah.

JILL: You don't seem the type.

BYRON: That's what everyone says. I should probably find another line of work but it's the only thing I know how to do. Well, that and being a porn star.

They laugh.

JILL: You're kinda cute, Byron, you know that?

BYRON: Well, like you said, the clothes haven't come off yet. We'll see how you feel about me when that's staring you in the face.

JILL: . . . When what's staring me . . .

BYRON: My naked body! When my entire naked body is staring you in the . . . you know?

JILL: Are you worried about your appearance?

BYRON: Well, that's one worry I have. The biggest worry of course is whether or not I'll be able to . . . you know? When they call "action!" I hope I'll be able to provide some.

JILL: Oh, you'll be fine.

BYRON: You think so?

JILL: Just keep looking into my eyes.

BYRON: Your eyes?

JILL: Yeah, it's what actors do when they're performing. They look into each other's eyes. They trust one another and they get their confidence from each other.

BYRON: Oh.

JILL: So just keep looking into my eyes. That's if you can see my eyes from where you are.

DAPHNE enters on the stairs.

DAPHNE: Okay, folks, we're ready for you.

BYRON: So soon?

DAPHNE: Yep. So, how ya doin' down here? Are ya getting acquainted? Gettin' to know one another?

JILL: Yes. Absolutely.

DAPHNE: Good. Byron? How's that rocket?

BYRON: . . . It might need a booster.

DAPHNE: All right. Let's shoot this thing!

DAPHNE exits up the stairs.

BYRON: Well, here we go.

JILL: Yep. Here we go.

BYRON: Good luck. I mean, break a leg.

JILL: Byron, don't worry about it. You're gonna be okay.

BYRON: You think so?

JILL: Trust me.

She takes BYRON by the hand.

You'll be in good hands.

JILL and BYRON exit up the stairs. ROLLIE enters from the wings.

ROLLIE: *(to audience)* So the first day of shooting was under way. Daphne had scheduled three days of shooting for the film. She wanted to give the actors time to "regroup" during the process. She figured there was no need for anyone to injure themselves, or render themselves unable to perform along the way. I won't go into detail about what too much sexual activity can do to a person. Although I think Daphne could speak to that. Meanwhile, in the days previous, Alex had contacted an "associate" of his who had agreed to distribute the finished product if he liked what he saw. Now all we had to do was produce the goods. I wasn't around for the shooting that first day. As I told you earlier, I was at work. I was helping Leonard prepare for his move to New York. He was very excited. He said they were doubling his salary. I was so happy for him.

Pause as he thinks about this.

So now we'll revisit that moment you saw earlier when you came in in the middle of the story. I'll stand off to the side. Just imagine I'm not here.

JILL enters on the stairs wearing a bathrobe. She is followed by DAPHNE, who carries a clipboard and a pencil. They are followed by ALEX who has a video camera. He is followed by BYRON, also wearing a robe.

DAPHNE: Jill, come back. Please.

JILL: He was looking at my breasts! He was staring right at them!

ALEX: I'm the cameraman. I was looking at every bit of you. But it was strictly on a professional level.

JILL: Yeah, maybe with your camera eye it was professional, but your free eye was checking me out.

BYRON: I thought he was checking *me* out.

ALEX: I told you, I'm not gay!

JILL: What is it with you and breasts anyway? Do you have a fixation about them?

ALEX: I'm a man. Breasts are the Holy Grail.

DAPHNE: All right, look, can we go back in and continue shooting, please?

DAPHNE drops her pencil. She picks it up.

JILL: Only if he promises to stop checking me out.

ALEX: I don't see what the big deal is. After we finish this thing, your breasts are going to be checked out by thousands of men. Hundreds of thousands! They'll be the World Cup of breasts.

ROLLIE: *(to audience)* I changed Super Bowl to World Cup. I think the World Cup of Soccer gets a bigger audience than the Super Bowl.

ALEX: Damn.

DAPHNE: What's wrong?

ALEX: I meant to say "Super Bowl" but "World Cup" came out.

DAPHNE: Well, the World Cup gets a bigger audience anyway.

ALEX: It does?

DAPHNE: Yes. Now would you promise her, please?

ALEX: Fine. I promise.

JILL: Thank you. How did they look, by the way?

ALEX: How did what look?

JILL: My breasts. Were they pointing out or down?

ALEX: Straight out. Like laser beams. I think you fixed my bad eye.

JILL: *(to BYRON)* Is that true?

BYRON: They were looking right at me.

JILL: Daphne?

DAPHNE: They held me spellbound.

JILL: All right, good. Let's go.

JILL, ALEX, BYRON, and DAPHNE exit up the stairs. ROLLIE speaks to the audience.

ROLLIE: Obviously everyone was a bit on edge about this. That's probably why tempers were short. I mean, we were all first-timers. We had never done this sort of thing before. The person I really felt sorry for was Byron. Now, let me talk to the men for a moment. Guys, you know what I'm saying, right? At the best of times, in a sexual situation, there's a lot of pressure on us. Tremendous pressure. I mean, if the corn don't grow they cancel the harvest dance and they blame us. And there are plenty of reasons why sometimes the corn don't grow. I mean, it doesn't grow automatically. It doesn't just shoot up because the farmer gets naked in front of it. No. Maybe we're tired. Fatigue can be a factor. Or maybe we've had too much to drink. After three or four beers, I swear that corn cob can turn to niblets. Or maybe it's just the pressure of expectation. You've got a woman expecting you to satisfy her desires. And that's nothing against you women. You have every right to expect that. But sometimes that expectation can chase that turtle right back into his shell. So, no one would have been surprised at all if poor Byron could not complete the daunting task which lay before him. Well, let's not keep you in suspense. Let's join our story now at the end of filming that day and we'll see how Byron did.

Beat.

You didn't think we'd shoot the movie, did you? You thought that something was going to happen and we'd change our minds. Maybe some money would fall into our laps and we wouldn't have to shoot it. Maybe Jill would back out. Maybe Byron would. Nope. We shot the movie.

ROLLIE exits to the wings. DAPHNE enters on the stairs. She looks stunned. ALEX enters on the stairs with the camera. He looks stunned as well. JILL enters on the stairs wearing a bathrobe. Her hair is askew. She looks satisfied. The three of them move into the living room and sit. BYRON enters on the stairs with a bounce in his step, smiling broadly. He is wearing a bathrobe.

BYRON: So, is that a wrap then? Is that what they call it? A wrap? Because I have some errands to run. I want to get to the supermarket before it closes.

DAPHNE: I should do that too. I suddenly have a craving for some corn.

ALEX: Byron?

BYRON: Yes?

ALEX: Byron, that was . . . that was magical, man.

BYRON: It was?

ALEX: Yes. You're an artist, my friend. A true artist.

BYRON: Oh, I doubt that.

DAPHNE: No, Alex is right. You were wonderful. Unbelievable. I don't know of any other man who could do what you just did.

ROLLIE enters through the front door wearing his jacket.

ROLLIE: Honey, I'm home! Hi, everyone. How did it go today?

ROLLIE takes his jacket off.

DAPHNE: It went very well, Rollie.

ROLLIE: It did?

ALEX: Extremely well.

DAPHNE: Exceptionally well.

ROLLIE: . . . Jill?

JILL: Hmm? Oh, hi, Rollie.

ROLLIE: So, it went well then. Well, that's good news.

DAPHNE: Yes, Byron here was extraordinary.

ALEX: He was an Adonis.

ROLLIE: Byron was?

DAPHNE: His performance was astounding. He was relentless.

ALEX: Stupendous.

DAPHNE: Not of this earth.

ROLLIE: Are you sure you're not going overboard, Daphne?

DAPHNE: No, not at all.

ROLLIE: Maybe just a bit?

DAPHNE: Definitely not. He was stunning.

ROLLIE: *(to audience)* I'm sure Daphne was exaggerating to make Byron feel good. I mean, the way she was talking, you'd think she'd never been around a good lover before, and, believe me, nothing could be further from the truth. No, Daphne was no stranger to fabulous lovemaking.

ROLLIE moves back into the scene.

DAPHNE: I've never seen anything like it.

BYRON: Well, I can't take all the credit for my performance. No, it's mainly because of the partner I had. I guess having a partner who excites you, who stimulates you mentally as well as physically—having a partner like that makes it easy to be a capable lover.

JILL: Aw, Byron.

BYRON: What?

JILL: Damn.

BYRON: What's wrong?

JILL: What's wrong? That's the nicest thing any man has ever said to me.

BYRON: Is that bad?

JILL: Yes, it's bad. I hardly know you. God! I met you three days ago. I go out with these other men for months. Years even. I live with them. I fawn over them. I turn my heart inside out for them, and they've never said anything half as nice as that.

BYRON: I'm sorry.

JILL: No, I'm not mad at you. I'm mad at me! I mean, I'm a nice person, right?

BYRON: I think you're a jim-dandy person.

JILL: I've got a lot to offer, right?

BYRON: From what I've seen, yes.

ALEX: I'll second that.

JILL: So why do I waste my time with insensitive jerks who don't appreciate me?

BYRON: You know why? You and me, we don't think highly enough of ourselves. That's the problem. No, you need someone to tell you just how terrific you are, young lady. And you need them to tell you every single day.

JILL: You're right. I do need that.

BYRON: Yes, you do.

JILL: Because I *am* a jim-dandy person, dammit!

BYRON: You most certainly are.

JILL: Thank you, Byron.

BYRON: You're welcome, Jill. Can I call you Jill?

JILL: As of today you know me better than my last boyfriend, my last doctor, and my last two dentists combined. You can call me whatever you like.

DAPHNE: All right, that's a wrap, everyone.

BYRON: *(to DAPHNE)* So, what time do we start tomorrow?

DAPHNE: Well, Byron, I think we got everything we needed today. I don't know if we need to shoot any more.

JILL: What?

DAPHNE: I don't think so. Alex? What do you think?

ALEX: I think I've got plenty.

JILL: What? No. Are you sure?

ALEX: I think so.

JILL: Oh come on. You don't need any more close-ups?

ALEX: Nope.

JILL: Two shots?

ALEX: Nope.

JILL: Long shots?

ALEX: No.

JILL: Please don't make me beg.

ALEX: Jill, I've got it all. In fact, I'm going to have to edit it down some. Byron, you're my hero.

BYRON: It was nothing.

DAPHNE: Oh, no, it was something. Believe me. It was . . .

DAPHNE gets a look from ROLLIE and stops.

BYRON: Well, I guess I'll get dressed then.

JILL: Byron?

BYRON: Yes?

JILL: Can we get dressed together? You know? For old times' sake.

BYRON: Absolutely.

BYRON holds out his hand to JILL. JILL takes BYRON's hand and they exit up the stairs.

DAPHNE: So that's it. We've got the movie!

ALEX: We've got it, all right.

ROLLIE: No. No, I don't think you do.

DAPHNE: Why? What's wrong?

ROLLIE: How does it end?

DAPHNE: How does it end? Ah, well, there's some spanking, a very creative use of your grandmother's armoire . . .

ALEX: And then the money shot.

DAPHNE: Right. The money shot.

ROLLIE: No. No, I've got your ending.

(to audience) Byron and Jill had given me an idea. Why not end our erotic film with a nice old-fashioned, romantic moment? Sure it was different, but nobody ever made a name for themselves without taking chances. Without showing some originality. And I wanted *Dr. Toolittle* to be a film we could all be proud of. And maybe if we grabbed the attention of the public, who knows, there could be a *Dr. Toolittle Two* . . . little . . . two. So, I explained my idea to Daphne and Alex, and then we called Byron and Jill back to shoot my new ending.

BYRON and JILL enter on the stairs. BYRON is dressed as a doctor and JILL as a nurse. They move to the front door.

DAPHNE: And, action!

JILL: I've got a lot to offer a fella, right?

BYRON: You're aces in my book, kid.

JILL: So why do I waste my time with a bunch of dime-a-dozen palookas who don't appreciate me?

BYRON: Lemme put you wise. Can I put you wise?

JILL: I'm standin' here, ain't I?

BYRON: You and me, we need some intensive care.

JILL: Why? What's the quandary?

BYRON: We've got a sickness and we've got it bad.

JILL: Yeah? What are the symptoms?

BYRON: Come closer and I'll tell you.

He pulls her close.

JILL: Why, Doc. Your heart's poundin' a mile a minute.

BYRON: Your pulse is racin' too, Nurse.

JILL: And you're runnin' a fever.

BYRON: And it's not goin' down.

JILL: So what's the diagnosis?

BYRON: Simple. We've got a bug called love.

JILL: Have you got a prescription for that, Doc?

BYRON: I sure do. Take these two lips and call me in the morning.

BYRON and JILL kiss.

And now let's go have a look at Mr. Walker's colon.

BYRON and JILL exit into the hallway upstage centre.

DAPHNE: Cut! And print it!

BYRON and JILL enter again.

BYRON: How was that? Was that okay?

DAPHNE: Perfect. Thank you. You two can get out of your costumes now.

BYRON begins to leave but JILL grabs his arm.

JILL: Did you get the kiss?

ALEX: Got it.

JILL: You don't need to shoot it again?

ALEX: Nope.

JILL: Maybe from a different angle?

ALEX: No, it's good.

JILL: I think we could do it better.

ALEX: No.

JILL: There's fifty bucks in it for you.

ALEX: Jill? It's good.

JILL: Oh, fine!

JILL and BYRON exit up the stairs.

DAPHNE: So, is that what you wanted, Rollie?

ROLLIE: It's perfect. The film says something now.

ALEX: And what's that? Have your colon checked regularly?

ROLLIE: No, Alex, the movie says something about self-esteem. About how a person with very low self-worth can be taken advantage of in this world.

ALEX: Great. A porn film with a message. That's like a strip joint with a dress code.

ROLLIE: You might be surprised, Alex. This could set a whole new trend in adult films.

DAPHNE: Well, I'm proud of you for thinking of that, honey. That's why I love you. Because you're so thoughtful. So caring.

ROLLIE: And don't forget about the great sex.

DAPHNE: No, I didn't. All right, who wants to celebrate with some wine?

ALEX: No thanks. I'm bagged. I'll come by tomorrow to edit the film. Can I use your big screen to do that? It would be much easier.

ROLLIE: Sure. No problem.

ALEX: All right. I'll just leave the camera here then. Have a good night, folks.

DAPHNE: Goodbye, Alex. Good work. Thank you.

ALEX exits out the front door.

Rollie? Should we open a bottle of wine?

ROLLIE: Sure. Why not?

DAPHNE exits to the kitchen.

(to audience) So, after everyone had left, Daphne and I sat down to enjoy a quiet evening alone. We talked about our lives to this point. About how after twenty-eight years of marriage we were still so very much in love. About our son Gerard and how we had provided for him as best we could and how we thought he had turned out to be a pretty nice young man. About how, with any luck, Leonard might suffer a debilitating stroke and force the bosses to take me to New York at double my salary.

DAPHNE enters. She carries a bottle of wine and two glasses. She sits on the couch and pours the wine into the glasses.

Yes, we passed the evening with many pleasant thoughts. And as the night wore on, and after we had moved on to the second bottle of wine, our thoughts turned to romance.

ROLLIE sits beside DAPHNE. He picks up a glass of wine.

DAPHNE: Cheers, honey.

ROLLIE: Cheers, babe.

They toast and drink.

I love you, Daph.

DAPHNE: I love you too, Rollie.

ROLLIE: And I'm sorry.

DAPHNE: Sorry? Sorry for what?

ROLLIE: That I haven't put us on easy street by now. That we still have to struggle to make ends meet after all these years. You deserve better than that.

DAPHNE: Oh, baby, don't be ridiculous. I never asked you to put me on easy street. We're in this life together, Rollie. We both got us to where we are. And you know what? It's not such a bad place. In fact, it's a damn good place. You've made me happy since the day I met you. Every contented breath that rolls off of these lips was put there by you.

ROLLIE and DAPHNE kiss.

And who knows, maybe this movie will put us on easy street.

They kiss again.

ROLLIE: Speaking of the movie, what would you say to you and me re-enacting a few of those scenes you filmed today?

DAPHNE: Really?

ROLLIE: Sure. Why not?

DAPHNE: Well, I mean you have had four glasses of wine.

ROLLIE: That's no problem.

DAPHNE: It's not? Because it has been in the past.

ROLLIE: Well, not this time.

DAPHNE: Sometimes two glasses can quell the uprising.

ROLLIE: Daphne? I can do this.

DAPHNE: All right, if you say so. Let's go, tiger.

ROLLIE: Grrrr!

ROLLIE picks up the bottle of wine and his glass and moves to the stairs. He waits there for DAPHNE. DAPHNE picks up her glass, starts for the stairs, then stops. She looks back at the camera. She moves to the camera, picks it up, and exits up the stairs. ROLLIE watches her go, and then comes back down the stairs and speaks to the audience.

Now, that seems like a good ending to the story, right? The film gets completed. Daphne and I go off to make love. And for the record, we *did* make love. But no. We can't end it there. What about the movie? Does it get distributed? What about Jill? Does she turn her life around? And Byron? What happens to him? No, too many loose ends. No self-respecting writer would leave an audience hanging like that. A good writer would tie everything up for you and put a nice little bow on it. So let me complete the story for you. Daphne and I attended the charity auction on the Wednesday of that week. Daphne's Pucci looked nice, and her dress got plenty of compliments too. Sadly, she didn't make any connections there as she hoped she would, but I ran into Izzy Dorfman of Dorfman's Costumes at the auction and he offered me a job with his company. And I wasn't even wearing an expensive gown.

ROLLIE puts his coat on.

So we fast-forward to one week later. I'm just returning home from my first day on the new job. So I'm going to go out now and . . . well, you know the drill.

ROLLIE exits out the front door, taking the wine bottle and his glass with him. After a moment he enters without the wine glass and bottle.

Honey, I'm home! It never gets old.

ROLLIE takes his coat off. DAPHNE enters from the kitchen carrying two glasses of wine.

DAPHNE: Hi, sweetie.

ROLLIE: Hi, babe.

They kiss. DAPHNE gives ROLLIE a glass of wine.

DAPHNE: So, how was your first day on the job?

ROLLIE: It was very promising, Daphne. Very promising indeed. There's only myself and one other person in the shop. Mrs. Feldstein. Yes, before long I'll be moving up to the top rung of that ladder too.

DAPHNE: You think so?

ROLLIE: Well, she's eighty-one. How long can she last?

ALEX enters from the kitchen. He has a beer in his hand.

ALEX: Hi, Rollie.

ROLLIE: Alex? What are you doing here?

DAPHNE: Alex came over to tell us about the meeting he had with his distributor.

ROLLIE: Oh, is it good news?

DAPHNE: I don't know. He wouldn't tell me until you got here.

ALEX: Yes, it is good news.

ROLLIE: It is?

ALEX: Very good news.

DAPHNE: Ooh. Tell us. Tell us.

ALEX: Well, I met with Vladimir last night.

ROLLIE: Vladimir?

ALEX: Yeah.

ROLLIE: Is he Russian?

ALEX: . . . Yes.

ROLLIE: Is he connected to the Russian mob? Are you getting us involved with bad people here?

ALEX: Do you want to hear the news or not?

DAPHNE: Now wait a minute, Alex. Rollie has a point. I mean, sure, it's a porn film, and it might make us wealthy beyond our wildest dreams, but we don't want that money to be ill-gotten gains.

There is a pause, and then the three of them break into hysterical laughter.

I'm sorry. Go ahead.

ALEX: All right, I met with Vladimir last night . . . and he loved the movie.

DAPHNE: He did?

ALEX: Loved it! He was over the moon about it!

DAPHNE: Oh! That's wonderful!

ROLLIE: See? I told you my new ending would work.

ALEX: No, he wants to cut that.

ROLLIE: He what?

ALEX: He said it was tasteless.

ROLLIE: Tasteless?

ALEX: Like Swedish vodka. His words, not mine.

ROLLIE: Well I don't know, Alex. I mean, we have creative control over the film, don't we?

DAPHNE: It's cut.

ROLLIE: What?

DAPHNE: I'm the director, Rollie. It's cut.

ROLLIE: I thought you liked it.

DAPHNE: I did. I thought it was insightful and poignant.

ROLLIE: So?

DAPHNE: It's cut. So, what happens next, Alex?

ALEX: Well, Vladimir will distribute two thousand copies to start, and if it takes off, the sky's the limit. We should start seeing a return in a couple of months.

DAPHNE: Oh, that's fantastic news!

DAPHNE hugs ALEX. ROLLIE looks to the audience, holds up his hand as if asking them to wait, and the doorbell rings.

ROLLIE: I'll get it.

ROLLIE opens the front door. BYRON and JILL enter.

BYRON: Hi there.

ROLLIE: Byron. Jill. Hi.

DAPHNE: Oh, you're just in time! Come in. Come in. You are not going to believe this.

JILL: What? What's going on?

DAPHNE: *Dr. Toolittle.* They like it. It's going to be on the market.

JILL: It is?

DAPHNE: Young lady, you are going to be rich.

JILL: Rich?

DAPHNE: Yes. You signed for points, remember? You'll be rolling in it.

JILL: Oh my God! I can get my car fixed!

DAPHNE: What are you talking about? You can get *everyone's* car fixed!

JILL and DAPHNE hug.

ALEX: And you're going to do all right too there, Byron.

BYRON: Why? I didn't sign for points.

ALEX: No, I meant all right in other ways. Once this film hits the streets, women are going to be clamouring for your goods. You'll be beating them off with a . . . well, whatever's handy. And I think you know what I'm sayin'.

BYRON: Well, that doesn't matter to me.

ALEX: What?

BYRON: No, I don't care how many women want me.

ALEX: Don't care? Are you out of your ____ mind?

He mouths the word "fucking" but nothing comes out.

(to ROLLIE) Stop that!

BYRON: No, you see, that's what we came to tell you. We came to thank you all.

DAPHNE: Thank us for what?

ROLLIE: *(to audience)* I don't say much in this section. I'm still stewing about my ending being cut. That's why I'm standing off to the side here.

JILL: We wanted to thank you for bringing us together.

DAPHNE: Bringing you together? You mean you're a couple now?

JILL: Yeah. We've spent every day together since we left here a week ago.

ALEX: And some nights too, I'll bet.

BYRON: Uh . . . no. No, we've decided to wait before we have sex.

ALEX: But you've already done it twenty-three different ways.

BYRON: Yes, but that was just having sex for the sake of the movie. We want our first real lovemaking session to be special.

JILL: *(to DAPHNE)* I think we'll start with position number fifteen.

ALEX: Ah, the Elastic Ballerina. My personal favourite.

BYRON: Anyway, we just wanted to stop by and say thanks. If it wasn't for you folks, none of this would have happened.

DAPHNE: Oh, I'm so happy for you. Would you like to stay for a celebratory drink?

BYRON: No, we can't. We have some calls to make.

DAPHNE: Calls?

BYRON: Yes, some clients we have to visit. Some overdue payments we need to clear off the books.

DAPHNE: We? You mean Jill's working with you now?

BYRON: Yes. I've found that a beautiful woman can be far more persuasive when it comes to collecting outstanding funds. She can utilize that remarkable charm of hers.

JILL: Oh, stop. By the way, Alex. That money you owe Byron? If we don't get it by noon tomorrow, you'll be lookin' for your kneecaps in your socks.

JILL exits.

ALEX: Now *that's* more like it!

BYRON exits.

Well, what do you know about that? They're in love.

DAPHNE: Well I'm not surprised. You hear about this all the time in film business, Alex. Two people work together on a movie and they fall for each other. It's commonplace.

ALEX looks longingly at DAPHNE.

Oh, knock it off!

ALEX: All right, I have to get going too. I've gotta get the final cut to Vladimir. I'll talk to you folks later.

He moves to the front door.

DAPHNE: Keep us posted.

ALEX: I will. Oh, I forgot to tell you. Vladimir liked the second movie too.

DAPHNE: . . . The second movie?

ALEX: Yeah. By the way, Rollie, I'm impressed.

ROLLIE: What do you mean?

DAPHNE: Oh my God.

ROLLIE: What does he mean?

DAPHNE: Oh my God.

ROLLIE: You mean he saw . . . He saw Daphne and me?

ALEX: Yeah. A bunch of us did.

DAPHNE: A bunch of you?

ALEX: Well, it was happy hour. The bar was pretty full.

ROLLIE: The bar? You showed it in a bar?!

ALEX: That's where Vladimir conducts his business.

DAPHNE: *(to ROLLIE)* I thought you erased that.

ROLLIE: I thought I did.

ALEX: No. I had it blocked so that nothing could be erased. And
Daphne? Kudos. I was moved. A couple of times. And then I
came back and finished watching. Yeah, Vladimir made prints
if you want a copy.

ROLLIE: Prints? There are prints out there? Circulating?

ALEX: Yeah.

ROLLIE: But, people will see us. We'll be recognized.

DAPHNE: No, wait a minute, Rollie. I don't think we have anything to worry about. Nobody we know is going to be watching a porn film. Right? It'll be fine.

ALEX: Yeah. I'm sure a virile young man studying hard to get through his first year of architecture wouldn't dream of watching a porn film. I'll see ya.

ALEX exits.

ROLLIE & DAPHNE: Gerard!!

DAPHNE: Well that's just _____ great.

She mouths the word "fucking" but nothing comes out.

What the hell?

ROLLIE: *(to audience)* The end.

ROLLIE puts his arm around DAPHNE.

Lights down.

End.

After twenty-five years in radio arts, Norm Foster discovered the world of theatre and began his legacy as Canada's most-produced playwright. He has penned an impressive array of plays, including a handful of musicals, that have been produced across North America. Norm lives in Fredericton, New Brunswick.

First print edition: March 2017
Printed and bound in Canada by Imprimerie Gauvin, Gatineau

Cover design & illustration by Patrick Gray

PLAYWRIGHTS
CANADA PRESS

202-269 Richmond St. W.
Toronto, ON
M5V 1X1

416.703.0013
info@playwrightscanada.com
www.playwrightscanada.com
@playcanpress